W9-DCU-891

CREEPY CRAWLIES

Ticks

by Megan Borgert-Spaniol

Note to Librarians, Teachers, and Parents:

Blastoff! Readers are carefully developed by literacy experts and combine standards-based content with developmentally appropriate text.

Level 1 provides the most support through repetition of high-frequency words, light text, predictable sentence patterns, and strong visual support.

Level 2 offers early readers a bit more challenge through varied simple sentences, increased text load, and less repetition of high-frequency words.

Level 3 advances early-fluent readers toward fluency through increased text and concept load, less reliance on visuals, longer sentences, and more literary language.

Level 4 builds reading stamina by providing more text per page, increased use of punctuation, greater variation in sentence patterns, and increasingly challenging vocabulary.

Level 5 encourages children to move from "learning to read" to "reading to learn" by providing even more text, varied writing styles, and less familiar topics.

Whichever book is right for your reader, Blastoff! Readers are the perfect books to build confidence and encourage a love of reading that will last a lifetime!

This edition first published in 2016 by Bellwether Media, Inc.

No part of this publication may be reproduced in whole or in part without written permission of the publisher. For information regarding permission, write to Bellwether Media, Inc., Attention: Permissions Department, 5357 Penn Avenue South, Minneapolis, MN 55419.

Library of Congress Cataloging-in-Publication Data

Borgert-Spaniol, Megan, 1989- author.
  Ticks / by Megan Borgert-Spaniol.
    pages cm. – (Blastoff! readers. Creepy Crawlies)
  Summary: "Developed by literacy experts for students in kindergarten through grade three, this book introduces ticks to young readers through leveled text and related photos"–Provided by publisher.
  Audience: Ages 5-8.
  Audience: K to grade 3.
   Includes bibliographical references and index.
  ISBN 978-1-62617-302-6 (hardcover : alk. paper)
  1. Ticks–Juvenile literature. 2. Bloodsucking animals–Juvenile literature. 3. Ticks as carriers of disease–Juvenile literature. I. Title. II. Series: Blastoff! readers. 1, Creepy crawlies.
  QL458.15.P37B67 2016
  595.4'29–dc23
                                    2015029886

Printed in the United States of America, North Mankato, MN.

Table of Contents

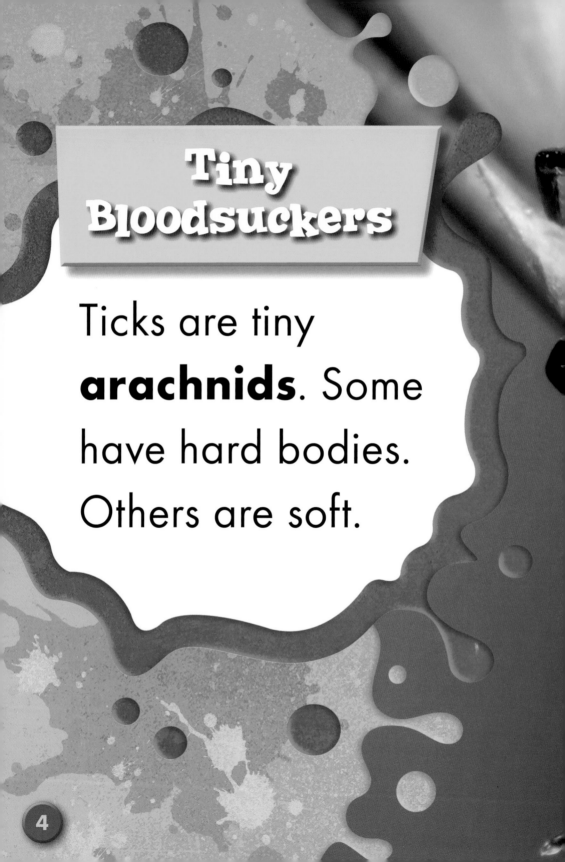

Tiny Bloodsuckers

Ticks are tiny **arachnids**. Some have hard bodies. Others are soft.

They live in grassy fields, forests, and animal **dens**.

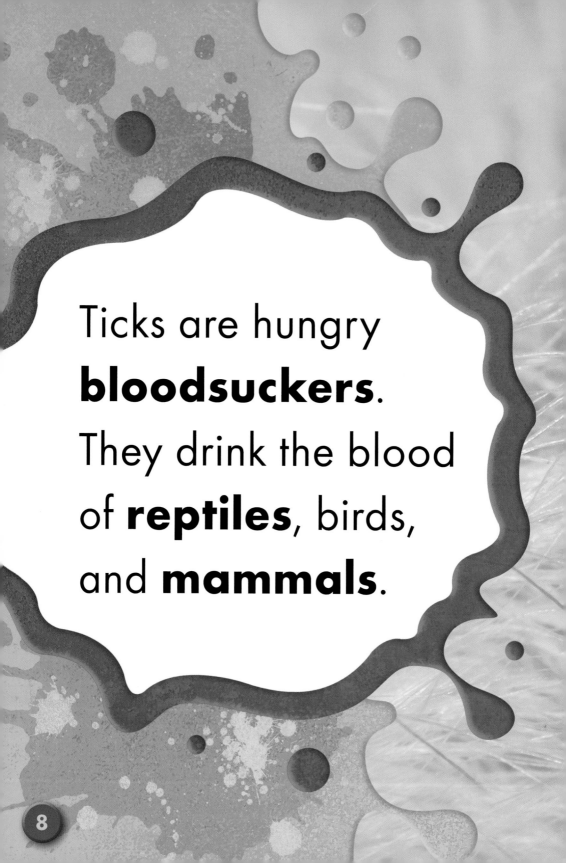

Ticks are hungry **bloodsuckers**. They drink the blood of **reptiles**, birds, and **mammals**.

Ticks crawl onto **hosts** as they move by.

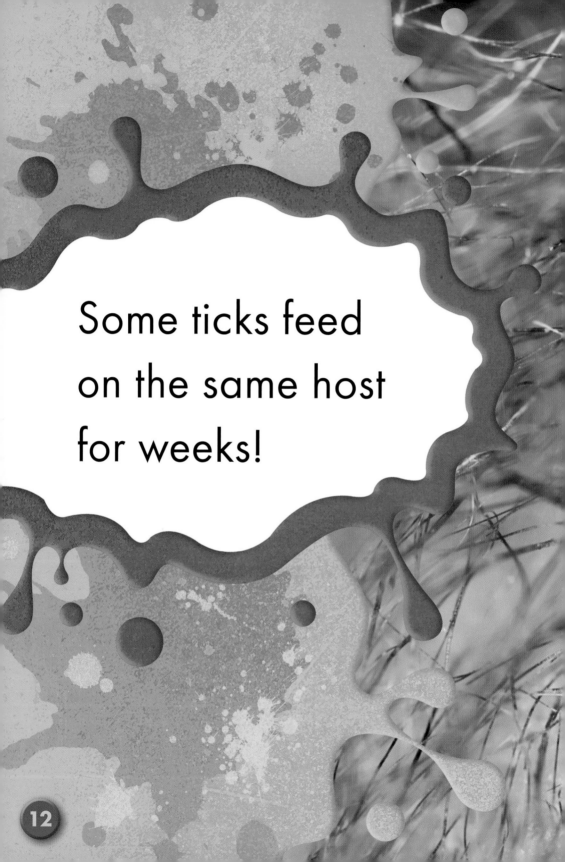

Some ticks feed on the same host for weeks!

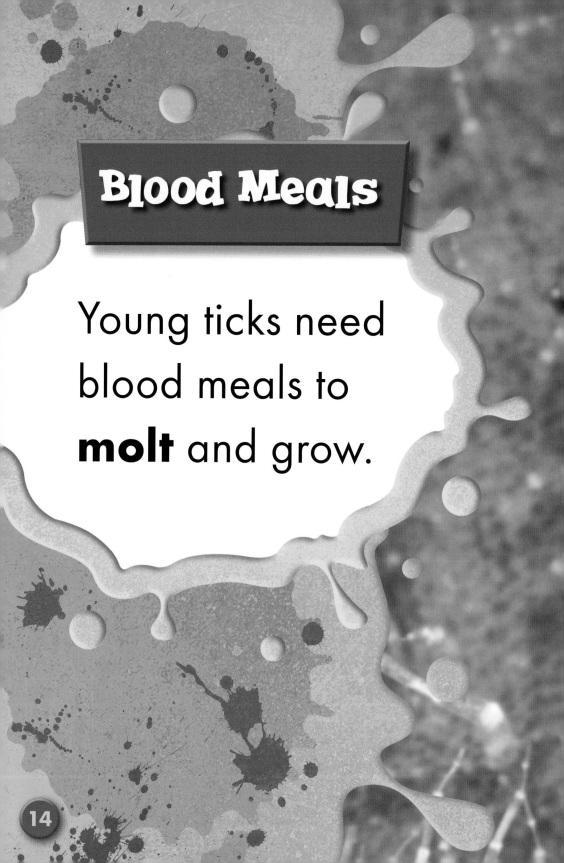

Blood Meals

Young ticks need blood meals to **molt** and grow.

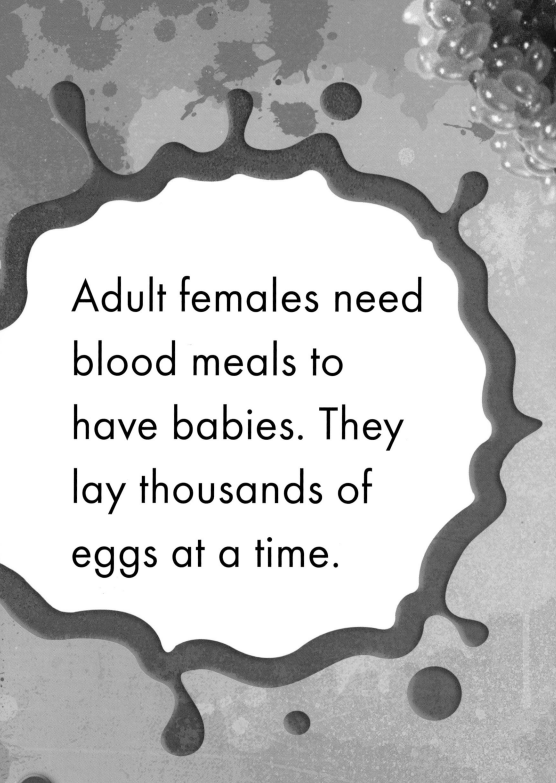

Adult females need blood meals to have babies. They lay thousands of eggs at a time.

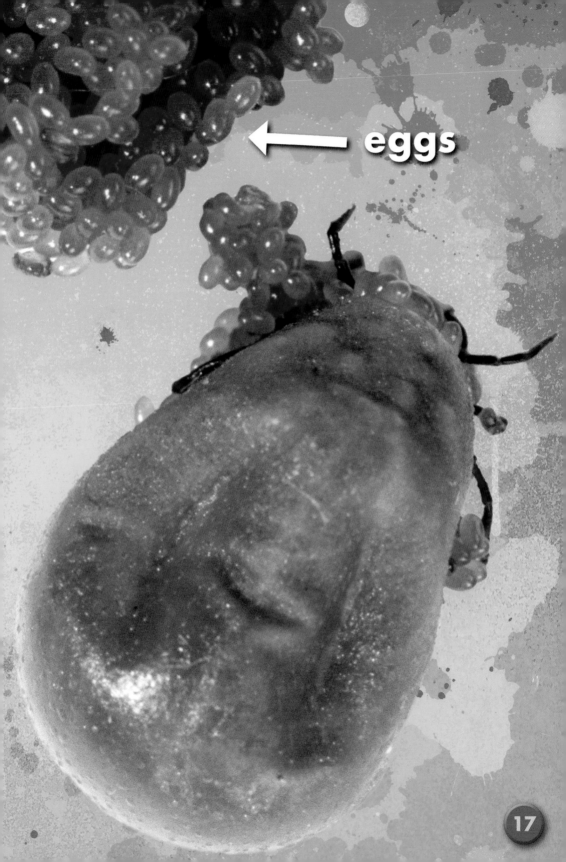

eggs

Sick From a Tick

Ticks carry sicknesses. Sometimes they give these to their hosts.

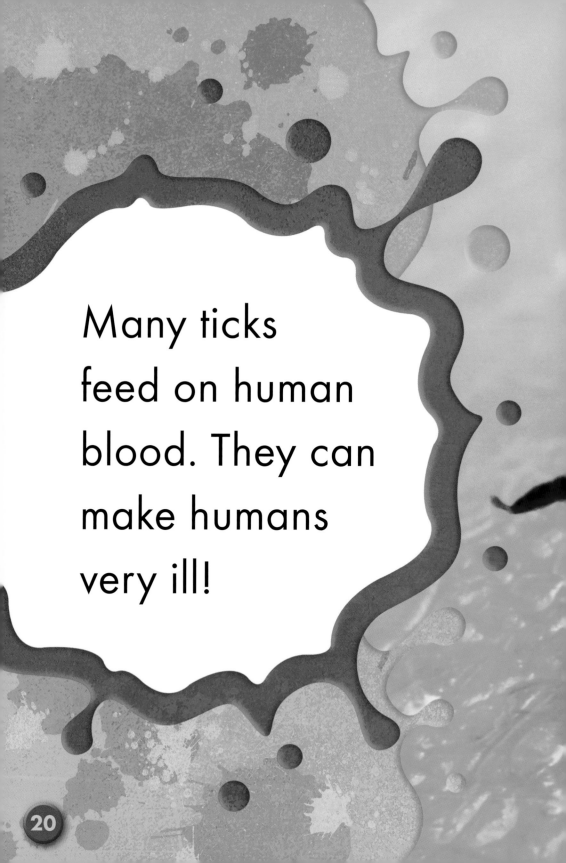

Many ticks feed on human blood. They can make humans very ill!

Glossary

arachnids—small animals with eight legs; an arachnid's body is divided into two parts.

bloodsuckers—animals that suck blood for food

dens—places where animals rest

hosts—the creatures that ticks feed on

mammals—warm-blooded animals that have backbones and feed their young milk

molt—to shed skin

reptiles—cold-blooded animals that have backbones and scales

To Learn More

AT THE LIBRARY
Arlon, Penelope. *Bugs.* New York, N.Y.:
Dorling Kindersley, 2011.

Fox, Nancy. *Hide-and-Seek: No Ticks, Please.*
New York, N.Y.: Morgan James Pub., 2014.

Merrick, Patrick. *Ticks.* Chanhassen, Minn.:
Child's World, 2007.

ON THE WEB
Learning more about ticks is
as easy as 1, 2, 3.

1. Go to www.factsurfer.com.

2. Enter "ticks" into the search box.

3. Click the "Surf" button and you will see a
   list of related web sites.

With factsurfer.com, finding more information
is just a click away.

Index